Table of Contents

Rourke
Educational Media
rourkeeducationalmedia.com

Can you find these words?

different

families

feelings

people

Alike and Different

people

People are alike.
They are **different**, too.

People have homes.

homes

But they are not all the same.

eyes

People have eyes.

But they are not all the same.

People have **families.**

families

But they are not all the same.

People have **feelings**.

But they are not all the same.

People have friends.

But they are not all the same.

Did you find these words?

They are **different**, too.

People have **families**.

People have **feelings**.

People are alike.

Photo Glossary

 **different** (DIF-ur-uhnt): When something or someone is different, it is not the same.

 **families** (FAM-uh-leez): Families are people who are related to one another.

 **feelings** (fee-lings): Feelings are thoughts or emotions you have.

 **people** (pee-puhl): People are human beings.

Index

About the Author

Pete Jenkins likes to be different. He likes writing books about all kinds of things. He doesn't like being like everyone else. He likes that he is special.

www.rourkeeducationalmedia.com

PHOTO CREDITS: Cover: ©sswartz; p.2,3: ©Rawpixel Ltd; p.2,9,14,15: ©RonTech2000; p.2,10-11,14,15: ©EvgeniiAnd; p.2,6-7,14,15: ©karelnoppe; p.4-5: ©Meinzahn; p.8: ©Jaren Wicklund

Edited by: Keli Sipperley
Cover and Interior design by: Rhea Magaro-Wallace

Library of Congress PCN Data
Alike and Different / Pete Jenkins
(My World)
ISBN (hard cover)(alk. paper) 978-1-64156-198-3
ISBN (soft cover) 978-1-64156-254-6
ISBN (e-Book) 978-1-64156-303-1
Library of Congress Control Number: 2017957807

Printed in the United States of America, North Mankato, Minnesota